FAIRY TALE MARKETING

FAIRY TALE MARKETING

BRANDY M MILLER

40 Day Writer LLC

For permission requests, write to the publisher, addressed:

40 Day Writer LLC

Attention: Permissions C/O Brandy M. Miller

2212 Cecille St.

Dallas, TX 75214

Or email: brandy@40daywriter.com

Fairy Tale Marketing / Brandy M. Miller

1. Non-Fiction-Marketing

2. Non-Fiction-Business Communication

3. Non-Fiction-Business Writing

4. Non-Fiction-General

5. Non-Fiction-Business Development and Growth

ISBN: 978-1-948672-26-9 (Paperback)

ISBN: 978-1-948672-23-8 (eBook)

Cataloging-in-Publication Data is on file with the Library of Congress

Printed in the United States of America.

First printing edition: 2015

Other Works By This Author

How to Write an eBook in 40 Days (or Less!)

Creating a Character Backstory

The Write Time: How to find all the time you need to write a book

The Poverty Diaries: Excerpts from the diaries of someone who's been there

The Secret of the Lantern: A Choose-Your-Path Adventure for Catholic kids

7 Steps to Change Your Life & the World

I Wish I Could Draw Like That: Life lessons on the road to becoming an artist

Turning Problems into Profits

The End of Purgatory (new adult fiction)

B.E. S.E.E.N. Study Guide: Bias Education and Techniques for Overcoming It

Dedication

Dedicated to those who made this book possible: to Joylynn Ross, who encouraged me to believe in the value of what I could offer; to Randy Ingermanson, whose Snowflake method helped me to see the connection between marketing and storytelling; to Dima Ermakov, who saw my storytelling abilities and helped me harness them in marketing; and to Jesus Christ, the Master of all Marketing and Word Made Flesh, without whom none of this would exist.

Contents

Foreword

Life might not be a fairy tale, but business sure can be . . . if you market it right. Otherwise, it can end up being a nightmare of a statistic. You the know the ones about only 20% of new businesses making it to the two-year benchmark, and less than half reaching the five-year milestone.

Thanks to my work with Author Brandy M. Miller – and Brandy working with so many of my clients – I'm not part of that statistic. And as a Black-owned, woman-owned small business owner, many people thought I was more likely than most to become one of those statistics. I can honestly say that had it not been for author Brandy M. Miller training and showing me how to get my clients to form an authentic emotional connection with me that led to genuine trust and connections, followed by sales, deals, contracts, partnerships, and relationships, I may not be able to write the business success story I'm able to today.

I always say that an entrepreneur and business owners first product and first marketing asset is their story. In this business-changing guide, Brandy proves this point by showing you the measure of success you can achieve when you actually make your story a product as well as use it as a marketing asset. And she's not just going to tell you to do it, she's going to give you the material to lay the foundation, and the bricks to use to continue to build upon. Because Brandy practices what she teaches and has experienced the wins herself that she knows you can achieve as well is what makes this resource so solid.

What I know for sure is that any entrepreneur and business owner who invests the time, money, and effort in this book as well as follows the formula, strategy, and system Brandy equips and empowers them with, they can prevent that nightmare of a failed, unsuccessful business from coming to past.

The six-figure business I once had and had always dreamed of started to feel like a nightmare I couldn't wake up from. Brandy came along with her magic wand and helped me turn things around. Okay, so maybe it wasn't as easy as the swinging of a magic wand. I'll be honest, though. On some occasions I did see stars – and not the ones sprinkled throughout fairy dust. But the ones you see when the truth knocks you upside the head . . . the hard truth, no less. And that, for me, is what the content in this book is; a hard truth I had to be knocked over the head with. But that wasn't what turned my business around for the better. It was me committing and being dedicated to taking action based on that truth.

Are you ready to take action?

Don't just read the book. If that's all you plan on doing, then I can tell you now that the information and tools inside are not going to work for you. Oh, they work. They work quite well. They just won't work for you if you are not willing to do the work to make them work for you.

What I learned in my 30 years of being a business owner is that there might be such a thing as getting rich quick. But if you are not willing to do the work it takes to go beyond simply maintaining and sustaining, but to grow, scale, and multiply, you can go broke even quicker. And not just financially, but mentally, physically, emotionally, and even spiritually broke(n) as well.   But no spoiler alerts here. I strongly encourage you to learn for yourself and earn for yourself using *Fairytale Marketing* as the vehicle to get you to your desired measure of success.

Before you hit the road to increasing sales and improving your business, I want to leave you with this final piece of advice: By no means with this book is Brandy selling you a dream, but what she is doing is helping you to achieve yours.

Continued success, my friend!

Joylynn M. Ross, Business Subject Matter Expert for National Government Agencies, Non-Profit Organizations, Corporations, and other Businesses and Organizations as well as the author of *Market Your Book: How to Earn a Living as an Author*

1

What Is Marketing?

B efore we dive too deeply into our fairy tale marketing journey, let's talk for a minute about what marketing is and its relationship to branding, promotions, PR, and advertising.

Branding: Making Your Company Recognizable

Branding boils down to two things: how you show up and the impression you make. Both matter.

How You Show Up

Your logos, fonts, colors, and the words you associate with you and your company: It's the external identifiers that help distinguish your business from every other business out there. It helps your ideal audience find you in a crowd. Just as the way you dress, how you carry yourself, the energy you bring, and the way you speak set you apart from the people around you.

The Impression You Make

This is where your reputation is built. It's everything people say about you when you're not in the room to hear it. It's based on how you treat people, how you conduct your business, and how people feel when they walk away from interacting with you.

Discover More About Branding

If you want to know more about how to build your brand, have we got a song and a course for you! Build Your Brand: https://youtu.be/V6XksL8Ro6Y is the song by yours truly, Brandy M. Miller, and the course can be found on our Path To Connections website: https://pathtoconnections.com/course/branding-for-the-small-business-owner/

PR: Letting Them Know and Like You

People do business with people they know, like, and trust. A PR campaign lets them know you exist and introduces them to you. Public Relations campaigns focus on developing and maintaining a positive image of the company in the minds of the public.

PR campaigns don't always focus on attracting customers. They might be designed to attract the attention of investors or win the support of government agencies.

These campaigns might look to build public awareness of the brand by drawing attention to charitable activities and events or sponsoring them. They might involve going on news programs or doing podcasts, blogs, and interviews in order to inform and educate the public about special projects or upcoming products and services that are in development.

When problems arise, PR campaigns help address those issues so the brand can retain goodwill in the eyes of the public. It's all about growing the public's trust and their awareness of what the brand offers while keeping a positive reputation.

Marketing: Building Trust and Demonstrating Value

Once the PR campaign introduces the individual, brand, product, or service and the public knows and like you, marketing continues developing the relationship by building trust and demonstrating the value of working with you. This can take the form of social media or blog posts, vlogs, or podcasts. The goal is to build up an audience, nurture the relationship with prospects, and convert those prospects into leads, and leads into sales/contracts.

Marketing does include advertising and promotions, but it is not limited to those things. Advertising and promotions are specific types of marketing.

Advertising: Giving People a Reason to Do Business with You

The goal with advertising is to give people a specific reason to do business with you. It can be about a giveaway you're doing or about a sale you're having. It can be about a product or service launch, a special appearance, or an educational webinar. The goal is simply to let people know what you've got and why they should come get it.

It works best as an accompaniment to the PR and Marketing campaigns because it takes roughly about 20 times of someone seeing or hearing about your brand and your offers before they are ready to take action and do business with you. Since advertising is often paid for, doing it without the branding and marketing can be a very expensive way to achieve the traction you want to get with your sales.

Promotions: Increasing Demand for Specific Products or Services

Promotions are used to increase demand for a specific product or service. They are used during launches of a new product or to boost sales of a product or service when sales begin to slump. They can also be used as door busters where you feature a premium product at an incredibly low price in order to get people onto your website or through your doors where they will (hopefully) spend more money on your services, products, and offers. You can also use promotions to attract people to an event such as a grand opening, anniversary, or informational seminar.

Fairy Tale Marketing: Providing the Messaging that Powers Them All

We've talked about the different types of activities that get the message about your business out there so the right people can find you. Fairy Tale Marketing powers them all.

Once you work through Fairy Tale Marketing, it's going to become part of your branding because it's the story you'll use to reveal the H.E.A.R.T. (humanity, empathy, authenticity, relatability, and trustworthiness) of your business. When used consistently, that story becomes your voice.

In PR, your story is crucial. It is what you'll use to get the invitations to appear on shows or in magazine articles. It's what you'll use to get the audiences to fall in love with you and your brand.

In marketing, your story is the cornerstone of all the value you deliver. You use it in your advertising and your promotions, too. In the rest of these pages, we'll show you how.

2

Why Marketing Efforts Fail

Companies that want to succeed know that marketing is an essential part of the game plan. It doesn't matter how good the product or service is if nobody knows it exists. Marketing effectively isn't usually cheap, either. Traditional mediums like print, television, and radio can cost thousands of dollars a month.

Paid online advertising can be extremely competitive, equal in expense, and frustrating in that your ads can be cancelled without any recourse and without any adequate explanation for why. Even the "free" advertising mediums like Facebook, LinkedIn, and Twitter aren't really free. They still require considerable amounts of investment in terms of time and resources as well as scrupulous adherence to their current advertising rules.

With all this money, time, and effort being spent on marketing, it's clear that businesses cannot afford marketing campaigns that fall flat. Yet many of them do. Here are the three mistakes most marketing campaigns make:

The Wrong Audience

No matter how compelling the marketing message, it will fail to achieve the desired results if delivered to the wrong audience. Children are not likely to find marketing campaigns featuring college students or college life appealing because it is too far outside of their experience and doesn't address the needs they face. Put that same marketing message in front of a teenager or a parent with older teenaged children, though, and they are likely to hang on to every word if the message appeals to them.

The Wrong Message

Even with the right audience, the wrong message will cause a marketing campaign to fall flat. The right message must address the most pressing needs of the audience with clarity, consistency, and cohesion. It must be easy to follow, easy to understand, and appeal to the audience's deepest desires. Last, but hardly least, the contents of that message must be believable.

The Wrong Delivery

Delivery of a great message can go wrong in many ways. The style of delivery can be wrong, with too many facts and figures produced without any narrative or visual imagery to help the audience remember the content.

The method can be wrong for the audience selected. Older adults are less comfortable with technology-driven delivery methods such as eBooks and are more comfortable with traditional methods such as radio, television, or print books.

The language used to deliver the message can be wrong. If the audience is largely college educated, using street slang isn't likely to appeal to them but will, instead, undermine the credibility of the message. However, when speaking with teenagers, street slang may be exactly what is needed to make the message relatable to them.

The Power of Stories

A well-told story delivers your message in a format that is easy to understand and easy to follow. Providing a narrative rife with visual imagery helps them remember the content long after they've been told the story even if they only hear the story one time.

It's a powerful method of reaching an audience in a way that appeals to them while developing a bond of trust that lends believability to the story, no matter how incredible the contents.

Fairy Tale Marketing

Fairy Tale Marketing takes the power of stories and weaves them into the marketing tapestry so that the marketing campaigns become more appealing, more powerful, and more engaging than ever before.

Fairy Tale Marketing isn't a dream or a matter of guesswork. It's a matter of thousands of years of human development, tapping into the science of how memory is constructed, trust is developed, and motivation to change behavior is formulated.

Ready to learn more? Keep reading.

3

It All Starts with the Brain

It's happened to all of us. A teacher stands at the front of the class spouting facts and figures about a subject for which we have no interest. We struggle to stay awake.

If we do not actively take notes, we won't remember much of that lecture at all. The reason that we won't remember, the reason that note taking helps us to remember, and the reason that we're struggling to stay awake are all connected.

When we listen to or read something that contains only facts and figures, the only parts of the brain that get activated are three tiny areas for language processing. That's it.

The rest of the brain is dormant, waiting for something to do. Note taking helps because it forces other parts of the brain to activate, so it helps more of the brain to wake up and get involved.

Memory and the Brain

The brain stores new information in our memories by chaining it to a past experience. If it can't find an experience we've had that is relevant, it tosses the information into a "junk drawer" for later review. While we are dreaming, including daydreaming, the brain rifles through that drawer and attempts to connect our experiences together with these new pieces of information.

That's why so many of our best inspirations come when we are dreaming. The brain finds an experience to chain that information to, and suddenly we gain a new insight into how the world works.

Those new bonds, though, aren't very strong. They need emotion and sensation to help superglue the old experience and the new together. That's what makes stories such powerful teaching tools and such powerful tools for getting your message out there.

The Science of Stories

While reading fiction stories, almost every area of the brain is lit up and active. That's because when hearing or reading about a sensory experience, scientists have found the portions of our brains involved in feeling that sensation are activated along with the portions that are involved in language processing.

In other words, when we read or hear about an experience, the brain responds just as if you were really experiencing that sensation.

It happens with emotions, sounds, sights, smells, tastes, and even tactile sensations. Whatever sensory experiences we read about are taken in by the brain as if they were lived out by us. Writing doesn't just have the power to give us information, it has the power to put us in the scene.

All those new experiences mean that the brain is provided so many more ways to file the information. That helps it absorb the information it is receiving with less effort.

> "Keith Oatley, an emeritus professor of cognitive psychology at the University of Toronto (and a published novelist), has proposed that reading produces a vivid simulation of reality, one that 'runs on minds of readers just as computer simulations run on computers.' - Annie Paul Murphy, "Your Brain on Fiction"

Emotion and Memory

Dr. James L. McGaugh, founder of the Center for the Neurobiology of Learning in California, discovered that rats who were stimulated with adrenaline remembered better than rats who were not. The same thing is true with human beings.

Intense emotions, combined with surprise, release adrenaline into the body, which embeds that memory deep within our brain and ensures that we remember it long after the event itself is over.

According to Jerome Bruner, a cognitive psychologist, a fact wrapped in a story is 22 times more likely to be remembered than the fact by itself.

A vividly told story that avoids clichés but uses sensory clues such as taste, touch, sound, smell, and sight to describe events or to package information will stay with us for years, long after we've stopped reading the story, just as a vacation memory stays with us long after the vacation is over.

That information becomes part of that memory and is brought forward with us each time we relive the experience. The subconscious mind does not have a sense of time. Events are relived as if they are happening in that moment no matter how far back in the past they occurred.

So, what is the best way to package your brand and business information, services, products, and offerings? Inside a story. But not just any story, your story . . . and your customer's stories when applicable.

4

How Stories Support Your Business

"The neural changes that we found associated with physical sensation and movement systems suggest that reading a novel can transport you into the body of the protagonist." - Emory University neuroscientist Gregory Barnes

O f course, that's not all that stories can do. Stories can build bridges of trust and incite empathy between strangers. Since our brains treat the experiences in stories as if they really happened to us, we automatically develop an emotional connection to the protagonist of any story told to us. If that protagonist happens to be the founder of the business, for example, people who read that story form an emotional bond to the business owner.

They literally feel as if they know that person. This phenomenon is known as narrative empathy. The reason for it is that oxytocin, the brain chemical responsible for trust and emotional bonding, is released during the experience of reading.

> *"even the simplest narrative can elicit powerful empathic response by triggering the release of neurochemicals like cortisol and oxytocin, provided it is highly engaging and follows the classic dramatic arc outlined by the German playwright <u>Gustav Freytag</u> 150 years ago." - Maria Popova speaking about a study conducted by Paul Zak, director of the Center for Neuroeconomic Studies and author of* The Moral Molecule: The Source of Love and Prosperity.

The Relationship between Emotions and Decisions

At one point in the evolution of neuroscience, the area of science responsible for investigating how the brain works, scientists thought that emotions cloud judgment and make decision making more difficult. However, in 1982, a patient of neuroscientist, Antonio Damasio, had a small tumor removed from his brain.

That patient's IQ had been in the 97th percentile. Only a segment of the emotional section of the brain was removed. The assumption was that this patient would now find decision making easier. What they found was the exact opposite.

The patient became a prisoner of logic and reason, unable to make even the simplest decisions, such as whether to use a blue ink pen or a black one. Our emotions come to our rescue when we are presented with options of equal value or similar quality, allowing us to decide based on our likes and dislikes instead.

A good story that creates an emotional attachment to you, your business, or your product makes it easier for the customer to choose you when it's time to buy.

Why Stories Work Better than Facts

When providing a customer with facts, you are asking them to alter their existing world view to accommodate the new information you are providing them. They have to then decide whether you are someone they can trust to provide reliable information. Then, they must decide whether the information you are providing them contradicts information they already believe to be true.

Changing our world view is not easy. Because the brain views our beliefs as essential to our survival, it naturally defends us against the work and the risks involved in making such changes. In fact, if the information provided is contradictory to what we already believe to be true, our emotions leap to our defense. They build a wall to protect us from what the brain perceives as an assault. Stories offer us a safe way to "try before we buy" the new facts.

During the story, we put aside our existing world view so that we take on the world view of the protagonist. We see things from his or her point of view. We then explore that world with that existing data set. It helps us to wrap our heads around new ideas and new information in a non-confrontational way. We know that we are free to leave behind that particular world view at the end of the story and take back our own if this new one doesn't work for us.

Creating a Demand

A recent study split students into two groups. One group read *Twilight*, a book about vampires. One group read *Harry Potter*, a book about witches and wizards. After reading the book, the students were asked a series of questions to gauge how much of the fiction permeated their world view. The not-so-shocking results?

The students who read about vampires were more likely to think about themselves as vampires. The students who read about witches and wizards were more likely to think of themselves as witches and wizards.

Our empathy with the characters in a story causes us to see ourselves more like the characters. We begin to want the things those characters want.

Increasing Value

Kyle MacDonald wanted a house but started with just one red paperclip. He put his story out there and told everyone that he wanted to barter one red paperclip for a house. It took him one year and 15 swaps, but he got the house he wanted. One red paperclip, one good story, and that paperclip proved to be worth hundreds of thousands of dollars.

Kyle's story worked because people became part of that story every time they bartered with him. In an ongoing project called <u>Significant Objects</u>, Rob Walker and his team buy objects for as little as $1.25 from thrift stores. They then hire writers - known and unknown - to write fictional stories around the object. A $3 bunny candle sold for $125 on ebay.

The stories didn't just increase the value of the objects, though. It increased the value of the stories, too. People were buying just as much for the stories as for the items themselves. The markup for the Significant Stories Objects? An average of 2900%. The right story attached to any object can automatically increase the value and worth of the item.

5

Understanding the Customer Journey

Before we learn to tell strategic stories that turn prospects into customers, customers into fans, and fans into raving fanatics that help you spread your brand's message all over the place, you need to first appreciate the journey they go on to becoming a first-time buyer. Your story is designed to move prospects along each stage of the buyer's journey to the point of conversion where they become your customer.

Unaware of – Or Unwilling to Confront – the Problem (Unaware)

This stage of the journey comes right before the prospect's true story begins. They are operating in their comfort zone, unaware of the possibilities or the problems on the horizon. As a result, they have no motivation to address those things, either.

The Confrontation with the Problem (Problem Aware)

Suddenly, the prospect is thrust into a position where the problem can no longer be ignored. That problem is face-to-face with them and toe-to-toe. The only thing left is to make a decision.

The Search for Solutions Begins (Solution Aware)

Long before the prospect reaches you, they're going to try a lot of different ways to solve their problem. However, because they don't know the truth that you're holding, the solutions they do find either aren't going to solve the problem or may even make the problem worse.

Your Solution (Your Solution Aware)

Because the prospect was not satisfied with the results they were getting from the other solutions they found, they kept looking and found you. Now they've become aware of your solution for their problem and what you can do for them.

Considering Their Options (Consideration)

Your prospect wants the best deal possible. They want to make sure they're making the right decision. They don't want to be disappointed by your solution. What they need at this point is emotional reassurance . . . a reason to buy. They're going to spend time making comparisons and looking for special offers.

Accepting Your Offer (Conversion)

Your prospect finally decides to accept your offer and makes the commitment to achieving their dreams. They transition from prospect to customer.

Experience the Benefits (Results)

Your new customer gets what you offer and they experience the benefits of it. They start getting the results you promised to deliver.

New Life (Transformation)

The customer's life is transformed by what they received from you and they are a new person. That doesn't mean they don't have problems anymore. It means it's time to anticipate those new problems and tell them how you're still the right person to help them solve those.

6

Structuring the Story

Remember: Your goal is to leverage your story to move your prospect along their journey. That's why it needs to have certain key elements in order to do this work:

The Problem

You introduce the problem to your prospects, letting them know not only why they need to face up to it and confront it, but why they need to do so now.

Their life may be comfortable at the moment, but you need to make them aware of any surrounding factors that could cause that to change at any moment. Alternatively, if they've given up on their dreams, you need to spark hope and inspire them to believe that the future their heart desires is possible.

The Mistake They've Been Making

Here's where you begin to grab their attention, making them aware of why the search they've been on for solutions is not producing the results they've hoped to get.

The Truth They Need to See

In order for them to embrace your solution, there's a truth they must see and accept before they can move forward. Revealing this truth will bring the aha! moment of enlightenment that will build more trust with you and position you as the right mentor for them.

The Solution You Offer

This is where you tell them what you're going to be able to do for them and how that's going to help them get the thing you know they want more than anything else in life right now.

The Obstacles to Implementation

Knowing a solution or even having it doesn't mean you're equipped or capable of implementing what you've got. You, as their mentor, need to know what obstacles they will face in the journey ahead and prepare them for it by listing out – usually the top five – obstacles they will face as they try to implement the solution.

Your Answers to Overcoming the Obstacles

What tools are you going to provide them with to help them overcome those obstacles? What actions are you prepared to take to help them get what they need and be sure the obstacles don't stand in the way of their success?

The Results They'll Get Along the Way

Tell them what it's going to do for them as they work to overcome those obstacles on their way to getting the results they want. This helps give them an incentive not to quit on the process before they reach their end goal: the transformation their heart desires.

The Life Transformation Waiting Up Ahead

This is the final outcome, the fruit of the journey they're on, and the reason to go through all the hardship, trials, and struggles along the way. It's the promise of the possibilities waiting for them if they stay the course, take you up on your solution, and leverage your answers to get past those obstacles.

Paint Vividly

Words are your paintbrush and their mind is the canvas. Your story creates the images in the mind of your listener. Paint it in vivid colors. What does it look like? What does it feel like? What does it taste like? What does it smell like? What does it sound like?

What texture does it have on the fingertips? The stronger the images you can create in the mind, the easier it will be for the customer to get into the story and to put themselves into the experience.

Storytelling Across the Pages

Once you have your main stories in place, these stories need to become part of everything you do. Every marketing effort, every time you share on social media, and on every page of your website.

If you make a blog post on your site, make sure the story fits your narrative. It needs to be a consistent and unified narrative.

7

Introducing the Characters

E very story has its characters, and your business story is
no different. The hero of every business story is the customer and not you. Every story you tell needs to, in some
way, help that customer see themselves as the hero and envi-
sion themselves reaching that dream solution.

The Hero

This is ALWAYS the prospect or customer. Not you. It's
their journey. You're just there to provide the guidance they
need to get done what they want done.

The Herald

The herald of the story is the person, situation, or event that forces the hero to confront the problem or brings their awareness to it.

The herald for a tire company may be that flat tire that finally forces your hero – the customer – to take the action of replacing their tire so they can get back to business and make sure their family continues having all the income they need.

The Mentor

You are the mentor. You are there to help your hero understand why the things they are currently doing to solve that problem aren't working for them based on your past experience. You're going to point them to the right solution, the product or service you are offering, and help them get past the obstacles that stand between them and their dreams.

The Sidekick

Their dream is their sidekick. It's the reason they are willing to fight through the obstacles and take the time to do the things they need to do in order to get the results they want. It often has a face such as a family, a husband, or a child.

The Minion

The minion of this story is whomever or whatever they're blaming for the problem or situation they face. This minion isn't the actual cause of the problem but a distraction from finding it. The minion keeps them locked up by preventing them from seeing and confronting the real problem.

The Gatekeeper

The gatekeeper of the story is the truth that they must find in order to unlock the solution. It's going to help them see past the minion's distractions.

The Negative Shapeshifter

The negative shapeshifter is the source of that lie they've believed. It's the voice of conventional wisdom. The thing that everybody thinks is true that actually isn't true.

The Positive Shapeshifter

The positive shapeshifter is a source that has been telling them the truth all along but they didn't believe what was being said because they didn't trust this character for whatever reason.

The Villain

The villain of the story is their fear, doubt, worry, anxiety, or past failure that's holding them back and keeping them from overcoming the obstacles. Your job is to help put those to rest so that the hero can prevail.

8

⌘

The Ultimate Fairy Tale
Marketing Story

People introduce Cinderella as a fairy tale romance. I'm going to show you that it's a fairy tale marketing story. Forgive me in advance for ruining your childhood. I promise you'll never see the story of Cinderella the same way again.

I'm going to use Cinderella's story to show you how all three pieces – the customer journey, the story structure, and the characters – combine to create an effective marketing story that lives on in the hearts and minds of everyone who hear or read it.

Introducing the Heroine

The story begins with Cinderella, whom we're going to call Cindy Ellers from this point forward. What do we know about Cindy?

She's young – late teens or early 20's at best. Slaving away at a job she may enjoy and which does give her room and board, but nothing beyond that. She yearns for a better life but doesn't see any way out.

Stage of the customer journey: Unaware.

Cindy's aware she's got a problem but she's in the un-aware stage because she's unwilling to confront it.

The Problem: Cindy's Terrible Life

Cindy wants nothing more than to escape the terrible life she feels trapped into living. She doesn't get paid, so she's got no money of her own, and the work keeps her so busy she doesn't have time to take on outside work. If she leaves, she loses her entire inheritance because it's all being held by her stepmother. What's a girl to do?

The Herald: Forcing the Heroine to Confront Her Problem

A herald arrives with an invitation to a ball at the palace. In that invitation is hope for Cindy: a way out of her situation and the opportunity to live the life of her dreams – if she can find a way to take advantage of it. This message of hope forces the hero to confront her problem for the first time.

Stage of the Customer Journey: Problem Aware

That invitation incited Cindy to hope again for freedom and to take action to try and make it to that ball.

The Dream: A Queen's Life

Cindy dreams of living a life of ease surrounded by beauty, with people who love her and subjects who appreciate her. In her mind, it's not possible. It's that mindset we must change.

The Sidekick: Prince Charming

Prince Charming represents Cindy's dream of being loved and cherished while living a life of ease surrounded by beauty. All good things, in her mind, come if she can marry him.

The Minion: Threatening the Sidekick

Naturally, because the invitation the herald brought is open to all unmarried women in the kingdom, Cindy goes to ask her stepmother for permission to attend. Her stepmother begins stacking up so much work for her that she's got no time to prepare for the ball, but Cindy's determined not to miss out. She keeps finding solutions to every obstacle her stepmother throws at her, but it's never enough.

The Negative Shapeshifters: Hiding the Truth

Cindy's three stepsisters serve as the voice of conventional wisdom, telling Cindy she can't solve her problems because she doesn't have any money or the right stuff for the ball. They're keeping the truth hidden from Cindy and are, instead, promoting all the things people believe that aren't true.

Stage of the Customer Journey: Solution Aware

Cindy's looking for all the solutions she can find to her problems, but her inability to find the truth is hindering her search.

The Current Results from Those Solutions: Being Taken Advantage of and Mistreated

Cindy's refusal to stand up for herself and express how unhappy the way she's being treated may be due to the fact she's tried complaining before and it got her nowhere or outright punished. However, it is opening the door for the stepmother and stepsisters to continue taking advantage of and mistreating her.

Cindy lacks a cornerstone of all negotiations: She's not willing to walk away and leave everything behind if she doesn't get her needs met. That refusal to walk away and lose it all rather than compromise on what she wants is what gives her stepmother power over her.

The Mentor: Matrona Goodson, Fairy Godmother

As the stepmother and her stepsisters depart for the ball in the family's only carriage, leaving a distraught and discouraged Cindy behind, along comes Cindy's Fairy Godmother, Matrona Goodson. Matrona is the CEO and Founder of Matrona's Market, which provides upscale products such as suits, shoes, and accessories, as well as transportation services for her clients to upscale events.

Matrona's been looking for a way to get her foot in the door in the lucrative Charming Kingdom market, and she sees an opportunity to make her own first impression and develop important connections by serving young Cindy.

Matrona listens to Cindy's story of events, empathizes with her situation, asks the relevant questions needed to get to the heart of the matter, and develops a winning solution for Cindy. Matrona is able to do this based on her own experiences as an entrepreneur.

The Mistake Cindy's Been Making: Negotiating from a Position of Weakness

Matrona clues Cindy into a key tactic in negotiations, and the reason she's been unsuccessful in getting her stepmother to treat her better: She's not willing to walk away and lose everything rather than continue to let herself be treated that way.

This leaves Cindy negotiating from a position of weakness rather than one of strength, as it reveals Cindy's lack of confidence in her own ability to make it without her step-mother.

The Truth Cindy Must Embrace: Her Confidence, Not Her Stepmother, is the Problem

Cindy could leave her stepmother's home at any time. But she'd have to leave behind her comfortable, familiar life in order to do it. She'd have to abandon her inheritance and step out on her own, facing poverty and homelessness. That takes confidence in herself and a belief she's capable of making it on her own that she currently lacks.

Matrona's Solution: A Time Limited Trial of Everything Cindy Needs to Show Up with Confidence

Matrona's business has a flagship offer that she extends to Cindy, which includes all the stuff she needs to go to the ball: the vehicle, the dress, the hair, the shoes, the makeup, and even the servants needed to make the perfect impression on Prince Charming during this time limited trial. The offer expires at midnight! If Cindy accepts the offer, she gets to keep the glass slippers as Matrona's free gift.

Matrona's Promised Result: Win the Prince's Heart and Secure Cindy's Freedom

With the right stuff, and Cindy's confidence, Cindy will have everything needed to get the attention of Prince

Charming and keep it. Taking Matrona up on this time-limited trial gives Cindy that once-in-a-lifetime chance to secure the life of her dreams.

The Villain: Cindy's Fears and Insecurities

Cindy's a smart girl. She knows the offer's a good one – a great one, even. But she's got a lifetime of fears and insecurities she's got to overcome to accept that offer. In short order, she asks Matrona:

- How do I stand out from all the other girls there?
- What if my stepmother and stepsisters find out I'm there?
- What do I say to a prince?
- What if the Prince and I don't have anything in common?
- What happens if time gets away from me and the trial ends?

Stage of the Customer Journey: Consideration

Naturally, Matrona has one advantage: No competition remains. Nobody else is offering to help Cindy, and her offer is both unique and a perfect fit for Cindy's needs. All she needs to do is help Cindy get past the obstacles and the conversion is almost guaranteed.

Matrona's Answers

She knows Cindy's got an incredible heart beating in her and all she needs to do is let the prince see it.

She spends time helping Cindy to see that her hopes for a brighter future don't end with the prince. She can take everything she's learned about cleaning houses and turn that into a business that will allow her to earn the money to buy her own palace and become the queen of it without needing a prince to get her there.

In fact, approaching Prince Charming as a business owner rather than yet another woman looking to make him the steppingstone to the life of her dreams is one of the best ways to set herself apart from the rest.

Nobody wants to be used. The prince doesn't want to be someone else's steppingstone to their dreams. He wants to be loved, valued, and appreciated for who he is, where he is, exactly as he is – just as Cindy wants that same thing. If she enters that room treating it as a networking opportunity for finding potential clients rather than a matchmaking event, it takes the pressure off the prince.

Matrona tells Cindy the truth. 80% of people in any given room are there to get something from others, not to give something. If Cindy becomes part of that rare 20% who is looking for a way to give to others rather than to get something for herself, she will automatically set herself apart.

Furthermore, all people have problems. If you don't know what you have in common with someone else, start there. Find out what their problems are and do what you can to help them.

Matrona says to Cindy, "If your stepmother and stepsisters find out you're there, fade into the background and look for opportunities to serve behind the scenes. They won't be looking for you there."

When the time trial ends, the only thing that will remain of the borrowed finery are the glass slippers, so Matrona reminds Cindy to be sure to keep an eye on the time.

Cindy's Positive Shapeshifter: Her Mother

Cindy's mother, who died when she was young, told her to see every problem in life as an opportunity. That's advice she neither understood nor took until Matrona helps her to see how the problem she faced of keeping house has now become her opportunity to build a business.

Cindy's Decision: Accepting the Offer

Equipped with the advice from Matrona, Cindy accepts her offer and sets off for the ball.

Stage of the Customer Journey: Conversion

Cindy decides to put Matrona's advice to work for her and to give herself an opportunity to live her dreams.

Cindy's Results: New Prospective Customers – and a Prince Searching for Her

Cindy achieves massive success at the ball. Her service attracts the attention of many people, including the prince. She gets carried away and almost loses complete track of the time. Sure enough, all the finery except the glass slippers goes away...and she loses one slipper on the steps of the palace.

That slipper becomes a calling card the prince uses to search her out. He can't believe his luck in finding such a smart, capable young woman and wants to secure her help running his kingdom.

Stage of the Customer Journey: Results

Cindy's Life Transformation

Cindy's new business takes off and soon she's able to buy her own palace. By the time Prince Charming comes knocking at her door looking for someone to fit into her shoes, she's able to meet him as an equal knowing that she controls the happily-ever-after outcome, no matter where she lives.

9

Creating a Product or
Service Story

S elling a product or service with a story requires a story
that makes the reader fall in love with that product or
service, attaching emotional significance to it so that price
no longer really matters.

Alternatively, it must show how that particular product
or service is the only product or service that will meet the
needs of our hero and help them vanquish the enemy and
overcome the obstacles to achieve the victory that eludes
them. I'll show you how to create both variations.

Creating the Product or Service Backstory

Use the story structure provided below to build out the
journey you went on to build your solution, and then help

the customer see what your solution can do for them if they accept your offer. This will help them understand:

1. What to anticipate when using your product/service
2. Why it's priced the way it is
3. The value the results bring
4. The transformation possible for them if they accept.

Sharing the Gift

This kind of story works well because it keeps the buyer as the hero of the story and points them toward your product or service as being the gift. Your role in this story is the herald, showing the hero the gift and teaching them how to use it.

The questions to answer when telling this kind of story are: What properties does the gift possess that is going to help the hero overcome their main obstacles? How is the gift activated or used? What steps must the hero take to claim the gift?

How can the hero be sure that this gift will work as promised? What are you willing to do to help if the gift should fail the hero? What precautions does the hero need to take in order to be sure the gift will work when they need it to work?

Joining the Quest

The "joining the quest" story invites the reader to become part of the story. It leaves the question of whether the quest gets completed up to the reader. An example of a "joining the quest" story is Kyle MacDonald and his red paperclip.

He invited the readers to become part of his quest to obtain a house by bartering, beginning with that single red paperclip. Each person who decided to go on that quest with him by participating in the barter or sharing the story became part of that journey and they shared in his victory when he finally got his house.

Their reward was the feel good of knowing they helped someone else along a difficult journey, a good story to tell, and an object of some value. Joining the quest stories work very well at product launches, for Kickstarter campaigns, or for any campaign involving a publicly announced goal.

10

Sharing Your Story

After you've created the stories you'll need, it's time to get out there and share them with others. There are many different ways to share, but we'll go over some of the most common methods. Choosing which of these methods to use will largely depend on your intended audience.

Websites, Video, and Social Media

If your audience is under the age of 64, the best method to share your stories is digital. Over 60% of people aged 64 and under use the internet regularly. The younger the population, the higher this percentage goes. This is almost universal, regardless of education level. 67% of those without a high school diploma use the internet regularly, and 72-73% of those with a high school diploma or more use the internet regularly.

1. On Your Website

You want a minimum of 400 words for each page, and one story per page. This 400-word minimum is actually set by Bing, Yahoo!, and Google. Any blog post or page with less than 400 words on it is considered "thin" by search engine algorithms. They treat it as spam.

Divide your website into three main areas: About You, About Your Business, and Your Products or Services pages. Focus on your persona story in the "About You" section. Focus on the story of your business on your "Why Do Business With US" or "About Our Business" section of the website. The products or services area of the site should focus on the products.

Landing pages, pages which you directly link to your pay-per-click advertising, should use the "sharing the gift" or the "joining the quest" story motif for best results. Every business website should have a regularly updated blog in order to keep the content fresh and prove to the search engines that your website is active. Your blog is an opportunity to showcase your expertise as an industry leader, educate visitors, and cultivate leads.

2. In a Video

Videos should be no longer than 2-3 minutes. If you need more time to tell your story, break the videos up into segments. Use YouTube or other platforms to host and then embed the videos back on your own website. You don't need super high-quality production on your video but do eliminate as many distractions from the background as possible.

More importantly, be yourself. Relax and talk to the camera as if you were speaking to a good friend of yours, one that you've known for years and are very comfortable being around. Try to rehearse your story elements enough so that when you get in front of the camera, you don't need to read a script to remember what you wanted to say. The more comfortable and relaxed you are when you're in front of the camera, the more appealing your story will be when you tell it.

For a product story, a video of the product that shows the product's dimensions and details can replace a video of yourself. For a service industry story, if possible, include the clients you've worked with for that particular service.

3. Social Media

Think of social media as a giant party. Stories are welcome there, but what isn't welcome is hogging the conversation or making everything about you. For this reason, a join the quest story is one of the best kinds to tell for social media. Using things that invite your fans to join along are more likely to attract fans and encourage participation.

Only one out of every 10 posts should be promotional in nature, otherwise you risk turning your audience off to your message completely. Sharing how-to, how-I-made, or how-to-benefit stories are also things that work well for social media.

LinkedIn is slightly different, as it's a social networking site geared toward business users, so everyone implicitly understands that they are there for business purposes. However, as with any social networking event in the business world, you still want to make sure that you are more focused on what you can do for others than about what you can get out of them. Use either the "sharing the gift" or the "join the quest" style of story for LinkedIn.

Television, Radio, and Newspaper

If your audience is over the age of 64, one of the best methods to share your stories is traditional media sources such as television, radio, or print advertising. You don't need to neglect the internet entirely, since 40% of those over the age of 64 regularly use the internet, but it shouldn't be your primary focus.

They prefer the comfortable and familiar, and most of them have a love-hate relationship with technology: they recognize its good points but they hate the learning curve required to use it. Effective ads in these mediums require choosing one message, one theme, and focusing in on it with laser intensity. Below are tips for condensing your story for television, radio, and print.

1. Television

Identifying stations in your area or program hosts that cover the kind of content you do is critical to gaining an invitation to interview on live television. However, as in the cases of most mainstream media, there is heavy competition for a limited number of spots and it can take a long time to get an "in" at the station of your choice.

This leaves you with television ads. If you're creating a television advertisement, you have 30-60 seconds to share the story. You don't have time for diving into the depth of your story. What you must find are those attention-grabbing highlights, sound bites, or memorable quotes that are part of your story.

This is where video footage of you and your business will silently help to support the story you're telling. Moments of extraordinary wisdom or insight, a pivotal success, a dramatic comeback after failures, all of these make great television ads because they get to the point and leave a lasting impression.

2. Radio

Sending a press kit sharing your story with a radio host that covers topics like yours is your best chance of getting a free radio interview. However, radio interviews aren't always easy to get and can take months to get approved. Radio advertising, though, is guaranteed time on air. If you're wondering whether people even listen to radio anymore, think of all the commuters who rely on radio to entertain them as they drive, and you have your answer.

You don't have the advantage of visual aids with radio advertising, so you're going to have to use your words like a paintbrush to create an image on the canvas of the mind, and you're going to have to do it in 30-60 seconds. While many of the same techniques you use with a television commercial will work with a radio ad, remember that it isn't enough to say that Bob's chophouse has great steaks.

You need to help them hear the sizzle and smell the savory steaks by the words you use. Description is everything in a radio ad. If you can get listeners to imagine themselves there, you've done your job.

3. Newspaper

Press releases are a tool you can use to share your story. You tell the story, you submit it to the newspaper, and if they have space or find your story interesting, they'll print it. It's a very good way to get your name in the paper at no cost to you. Because of the high volume of competition for these kinds of stories, it isn't always possible.

The other way to get in is to use a print advertisement. Print advertisements rely heavily on the images to tell the story. Text is secondary. As you're designing the print advertisement, avoid putting too much text in any one area. Text requires the brain to work hard, converting the symbols to meanings and analyzing those meanings in conjunction with the other pieces of text and the visual support to arrive at the intended message.

When the eyes encounter a "wall of text," which is an area that is almost completely text, it will ignore most of that and refocus on the visual imagery because that's easier for it to digest. A good print advertisement uses just enough text to drive home a single message and uses the imagery to do the majority of the storytelling.

Books, Presentations, and Webinars

Books, presentations, and webinars may sound like they belong strictly in the realm of coaches and gurus, but almost any business can benefit from these kinds of products. Taking the time to produce a book in which you share the insights you've gained from your business, or to give people advice that will help them, can give you instant authority in the business community and grant you an automatic advantage over your competition.

This same advice book can then be broken down into segments and used as the outline for presentations and webinars. You can use these books, presentations, and webinars to generate passive streams of revenue, to attract new clients or customers, or even as special offers to reward existing clients, boosting loyalty and increasing the likelihood they'll do more business with you in the future.

11

⬧

Getting Started

If you've read this and you're convinced, like I am, that Fairy Tale Marketing is the way to go, there's no better time to start sharing and marketing your story than today. There are two options available for you to get started:

Know How to Write Copy That Sells?

If you're the creative type who is good at crafting stories, get started working on those stories today. Write out your business story in long form, between 10-15 pages is enough, and then use the long form to write a condensed version of 3-5 pages, 1-2 pages, and a then a single page. Use the one-page version for your "about our company" page on your website and for print materials such as brochures.

You'll also use that one-page biography to submit for speaking engagements and press releases. The one-to-two-page stories can be saved for magazine articles and submissions that require a longer length. Your three-to-five-page stories are considered short stories. Your 10-15-page story is one you can turn around and offer as a free eBook, especially if you pack that story with helpful lessons and tips. Do the same thing with your marketing story and create a story for each product or service you offer.

Attend the Next B.O.S.S. Workshop

Don't know how to write your story in a way that will help you sell yourself, your products and services, your brand, or your business? No worries.

Path To Connections offers regular B.O.S.S. Business of Strategic Storytelling workshops that will teach you how. Participants get access to our B.O.S.S. App. Input the data, hit the generate button, and get a rough draft to use for yourself, your brand, your products, and services, or even your blogs.

Visit https://pathtoconnections.com/b-o-s-s-workshop/ and register now.

Use Our B.O.S.S. App

Want more automation in your storytelling but don't want to use AI? You're in good hands. We've developed an APP to help you with that. Those who register for the B.O.S.S. workshop get free access to our app.

Our Services

At Path To Connections, you'll find a variety of services designed to help entrepreneurs and businesses.

Part I. C.A.P. (Contract and Application Preparedness Program)

C.A.P. Part I provides the support that businesses need to obtain grants, win contracts, secure loans, acquire investments, and land the opportunities that allow them to accelerate, grow, and scale their businesses.

It starts with B.O.S.S., then follows up with L.I.P.P. (Legal and Intellectual Property Protection), moves into R.A.P. (Requirements and Paperwork), then goes on to D.A.R.T. (Documentation and Referrals, Testimonials), and ends with UPLOAD. During UPLOAD we literally work with you to get the paperwork uploaded to the portals or mailed to the opportunity on time.

Part II. C.A.P. (Contract Accountability Program)

C.A.P. Part II provides the support entrepreneurs/businesses need once they've obtained the grant, won the contract, secured the loan, acquired the investors, and landed the opportunities so they can deliver what's expected on time and on budget.

We get business owners M.A.P. (Marketing and PR) Ready, teach them how to L.E A.D. (Leaders and Executives Accelerated Development), and help them L.E.A.P. (Leaders and Executives Accountability Program) into action. Then we finish with making them the B.O.S.S. of their industry by helping them share the success stories of what their partnership did for their organization and the community in which it resides.

Training Programs

We also offer a host of training programs:

5 Steps to Get Anyone to Lean in and Listen to You: Helping small business owners and professionals prepare for success in any event they attend or meeting room they step into

Branding for the Small Business Owner: Helping small business owners build a brand no matter what's in their bank account

B.E. S.E.E.N. Bias Education and Techniques training: Helping business owners, professionals, educators, and students understand the causes of bias and provide them techniques for overcoming it

Magnetic Thought Leadership Training: Helping small business owners and professionals gain the cooperation of those around them in achieving their visions, building their dreams, and accomplishing goals – without the stress.

Turning Problems into Profits: We help aspiring entrepreneurs, small business owners, and major corporations alike learn to take the problems they've learned how to solve and turn them into profitable solutions that can help them pivot in tough times, expand profitability in lean times, and start successful business ventures with minimal up front investments. You can get access to free self-paced online training for this through Loving Catholicism by visiting https://lovingcatholicism.com/course/turning-problems-into-profits

If you decide that you want to take storytelling to the next level and write and publish a book, visit www.PathToPublishing.com for author assistance and literary and publishing services.

Award-winning author and international speaker, Brandy M. Miller began her education in marketing while working in the marketing department of a Fortune 500 company. She left that company to start her own and discovered that marketing to a cold audience with no money was a very different beast than marketing to a pre-built audience with a well-established brand and $2 billion dollars a year to spend on the task.

Author Brandy M. Miller
copyright 2022 Tiffany E. Rodolico

It was during her struggles to learn how to market on a $0 marketing budget that she uncovered the connection between storytelling and marketing. She would later test and refine her copywriting skills by assisting LeBlond Media with developing paid marketing campaigns for well-funded startup companies in Silicon Valley. She was able to help these companies increase their return on ad spend as much as 800% in the case of Google Advertising and increasing the ad account spend by thousands of dollars per month.

Today, she is the co-founder of Path To Connections as well as the Director of Program Development and Coordination for Path To Publishing and the Chief Acquisitions Editor for PTP Press, the primary divisions of End of the Rainbow Projects, Inc. She works alongside founder and CEO, Joylynn M. Ross, to serve their clients.

Connect with Brandy Online

Email: brandy@pathtoconnections.com
or brandy@40daywriter.com
Website: https://40daywriter.com
or https://pathtoconnections.com
Twitter/X: @WriterBrandy
Instagram: @DesignerBrandy
LinkedIn: https://www.linkedin.com/in/brandymmiller/
Facebook: https://www.facebook.com/AuthorBrandyMiller